A
HANDFUL
OF
STARS

Monarch Publishing, 2018
www.monarchbookstore.com

Cover and Interior Art by Nicole Frenette

To my mother,
I miss you.

To my father and brother,
I love you.

These words are mine to feel
but I will share them with you.

the falling.

Let me tell you a little bit about falling. There you are, standing at the edge of the highest mountain with your fists held tightly by your sides as you stare at what lies before you. It is darkness. The air is bleak but every now and then a harsh wind brushes against your skin and you sway your head in the direction it takes you, bristling thin strands of your hair that hasn't been combed for days because you no longer care about how you look. Or what you feel. Or the things your mind was telling you every step along the way towards the tall mountain facing an empty blackness that will suck you in and throw you back out as though you are nothing but a thin crinkle of dust. You also don't care about the things you said to your reflection in the mirror that morning when, once more you woke up with a stiff neck from a night of restlessness to a succession of unreplied messages from the one person that mattered the most, a throbbing heart and an ache at the pit of your stomach because you forgot to eat last night. Again. Those pep talks to your weary-eyed, tired and crumbling reflection in the mirror don't mean anything now as you face the edge of this mountain of feelings and empty wishes and ideas and broken dreams that you have created for yourself. And you block every single thing out as you stand at the edge of the highest mountain with your fists held tightly by your sides and you stare at what lies before you. It is darkness. And you let yourself fall.

I have spent
my whole life
being told
I am too much
of everything
by people who
have only known
how to live
in mediocrity.

It is not hard
to love me,
it is hard
to look at
every scar
every wound
every tear
and then
to love me.

Sometimes
it is the
right decision
that is the hardest
to make
it is doing
the right thing
that hurts the most.

Have you ever
wondered
that perhaps you
too have taught others
some lessons
good and bad
broken their hearts
hurt their soul
left them feeling cold,
have you?

I die a little
on the inside
when I think
about
every single time
that I neglected
myself.

One day
you will be
with someone
who will know
that you have
always been
worth fighting for,
and he will
never let go.

I am not the one
who is made
to save you
I am not the one
who is made
to cure
I am only a passerby
in your journey
I am not the one
you have been waiting for.

Pray,

pray
that the strength
to ask for
forgiveness
finds them before
the strength
to give
finds you.

It is in silence
that I feel you the most.

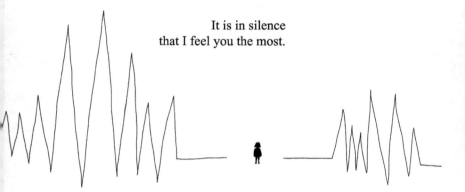

These days even falling stars
hide themselves from
eyes closed and
palms held together
in hope that
they will make those
wishes come true
that have been
living in a heart
stuck on
the idea of forever.

It hurts the most
when they know
just how broken
you already are
but still
they choose
to break you more.

I am so scared
of my heart
and
how much
it is capable
of loving you.

The angel and the devil
both reside within you,
when I look at you
and see one
it is hard to believe
that the other exists.

He tells me that
my smile is beautiful
and my eyes
shine brighter than the stars
he mentions
the colour of my hair
the softness of my skin
the scarcity of visible scars
but he does not notice
a whole universe hidden
deep within me,
and that is how I know.

Restless nights
are a gentle killer.

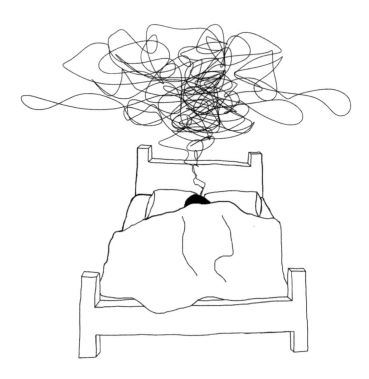

I know you wanted
her to trust you
but you never gave her
a reason to.

And the next time you ask
me whether I am okay
I will not lie and say yes
I will not bottle up those tears
behind a smile that never
reaches my eyes
instead
I will shake my head
and curl up into a ball
I will let my emotions paint my
face and I will let my heart weep
and I will let you
come to me then
I will let you hold me in
a tight embrace
the way you always
do in my head.

Oh, how
I wish
we were as good
at mending
our hearts
as others are at
breaking them.

I have given up
hope of finding him
in a generation
that does not know
the meaning of
loving someone's soul.

My mother always
believed in giving her
all to everything that
she loved,
I do not have
the same heart as her
and so
I choose to keep
the most valuable pieces
to myself,
I guess that is why
every time I break
I only lose parts
where I would have
otherwise lost wholes,
my mother would not
be pleased
'you are not putting
your heart into it all'
she would say,
but she is not here
anymore
and every day
I am lessening
little by little too.

Over time
everything slowly
fell back
into place
but this anxiety
just never
never left.

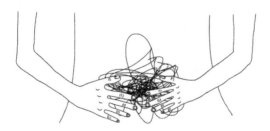

Dear heart,
I need you
to listen to me
I need you
to stop feeling
things
for a while.

And when
you finally walk down
the lane that
many have trod on
bracing your soul
feelings out of control
nervous tingles
dancing in your stomach
as you carry your heart
in your palm
ready to give to me,
I will say just one thing,
I told you not to
fall in love with me.

I am not here
to give a justification
for my emotions
I am only here
to share them with you.

It is not love

if it fills your heart
with pain instead of
warmth each night,

It is not love

if you can't eat,
sleep, think or breathe
not because you
are happy
but because you
hurt too much,

It is not love

if, instead of
making you
strong
it makes
you weak,

It is not love

if it causes you to
appreciate yourself less
and them more,

And it is never love

if you have to fight
to be loved.

They will always tell you
'anyone will be lucky
to have you'
until they realise
it is them that
your heart wants.

I wish I could
tell you
the reason for
my hesitance
the reason for
every single no
but sometimes
my scars manage
to say it better
than me.

And there you are
standing tall
quietly fighting
their battles
carrying the weight
of their worlds
on your tiny shoulders,
not thinking about
what will happen
when your own world
tumbles over
not worrying about
when that happens
who will fight for you?

You need to stop
seeing them
as wholes
when they see you
as nothing
but broken pieces.

You give
and give
and give
and never ask
for anything
in return.

It is these things
called feelings
that mess us up
the most.

If you meet me
and think that
I am falling
and hurting
and feeling for you
and if you cannot
hold me
or catch me
or be there for me
then please
just walk away.

Sometimes
it takes
receiving love
from the wrong
person
to realise
that the one you
were waiting for
was not the
right person.

Losing a parent
is like losing a limb
your sight
your ears
your smile
your heart
your soul
and still being expected to
walk, see, hear and breathe
as you did before,
and still being expected
to live as you did before.

I wish
I could hold you tight
one last time
so that you would not
want to let go.

If only
staying in love
was as easy
as falling.

This problem
is mine to bear
and I will
deal with it
myself.

'I love you'
he says
but it does not
sound right
coming from
the wrong person.

You read my poems
and remember her
poems which I write
after I remember you
and I cannot help
but hurt
when I try to stop
writing those
very poems
that bring me closer
to you
because they
take you closer
to her.

I fall
for your soul
more
and
more
with each
passing day.

You
   need
      to stop
         chasing
            feelings.

Sometimes
it is not the weight
of past experiences that
end up burdening us
it is the weight of our
broken hearts.

Look in the mirror
and whisper to your reflection,

I am not incomplete
without him.
I am not incomplete
without him.
I am not incomplete
without him.

And sometimes
I wonder why
the brightest stars
are the loneliest.

I gave you
as many chances
as I should have
given myself
and that was why
you won
and I lost.

I hurt them
they hurt me
it is a constant cycle
an ongoing interaction
of breaking
and being broken
of tearing
and getting torn
of wounding
and being wounded,
but I do not know if
I can play this game
any longer.

When you worry more
for someone else
and less for yourself
when their tears
make your heart hurt
when you smile seeing
them happy
when their struggles
tire you
when their pain
tears you in two,
you know you are
in love.

Hold my hand
let me take you
out of
her misery.

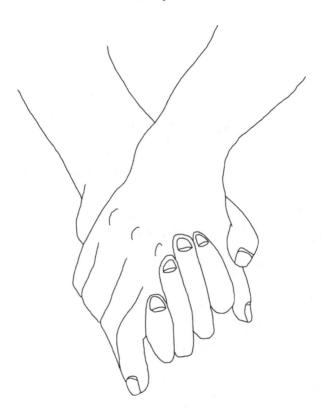

To every single person who
was taken by my light from afar
who felt that I was made of just
magic and love
who never understood that
these bones ran dry
and this heart hurt
who never thought about
the ache in my chest
hidden deep within
but when you realised that I
was not the beautiful picture
you painted me to be,
you were the first to leave.

It so exhausting
having to guess
all the time
what you mean
when you say
things to me.

- *communication in my generation.*

The pain
when it comes
and you are all
too familiar
with the way
it makes you feel
the way it hurts
the way it breaks
you in two
the pain
when it comes
it reminds you of
everything that
scared you
about falling.

I no longer know
how I feel about you.

It is a weird entity,
love
you do not realise
that you fell in it
until you find yourself
trying so hard
to get out of it.

God gives you
every single thing
that you want
just not when
you want it
but when he thinks
you need it.

My heart is too
hopeful
my mind too
practical
and I
am constantly
drifting
between the two.

Stop waiting
for him to
give you the
attention
that you
should be
giving
yourself.

I gave you my trust
to respect it
to protect it
to keep it safe
but you
framed it on the wall
as something to show off
kept it on the mantelpiece
with all of the other things
you had long forgotten about,
tossed it in the bin
threw it on the way to another
journey to trust you
wanted to make
and you never looked
back again.

You are
and always
will be
my exception.

Why is it that those we love
cannot love us back
why is it that we cannot love
those who love us
back
why do we have
to hurt someone
who would
do anything for us
why do they have
to hurt us
when we would do
anything for them.

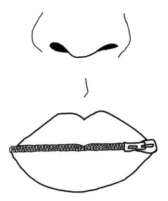

I fall a lot more
for what people
do not say
than what they do.

Every single time
I tell him that
he failed to understand
my affection
and he tells me that
I failed to understand
his friendship.

- unrequited love.

It is this heart,
it is this heart
that always
gets me
in trouble.

And that is the sad part,
sometimes
we hurt people
knowingly
because we
cannot give them
what they want
even if we
would like to.

I know
I give too much
importance to
the wrong people
and not enough
to the right.

Be honest with me,
tell me you do not feel
the same way
and I swear
I will walk away
but just
be honest with me.

No matter how
far I come
I still find myself
tearing up for
the girl
who once
believed in you.

I have to admit,
all of my love poems
are about you.

That little
beating heart
of yours
speaks of truths
that your lips
fail to voice,
that little
throbbing soul
of yours
speaks of pain
that your eyes
fail to hide.

Some days
are emotionally
draining and
some nights are.

There should always
be a limit
to how many times
you are willing
to forgive someone.

I will never understand
how it is possible for us
as humans
to crave someone's
affection
so much to a point
that it slowly kills us
every single day
and then to wake up
one morning
and not feel a thing.

Love was not made
for the fainthearted.

I do not know
if I am hurt
because of
the way
you treat me
or because
of the way
that I think
you treat me.

Those night-
whisper
conversations
are the ones
that I will
remember
the most.

It is so tiring,
believe me
it is so tiring
feeling things
this deeply
all the time.

Your only problem was
that you still wanted to
hold onto her
while you were too busy
exploring
all of your other options.

- relationships in my generation.

Love is such a strong word
and only time will
show you
that sometimes
you do not love
a person,
you love the
idea of them
which is really not
them at all.

I do not wish
for you to go through
the same things you
put me through,
what kind of monster
would that make me?
wishing harm
for someone I claimed
to care about, but then
what kind of monster
did it make you?
for hurting me
when you said that
you would not.

It really is a heavy battle,
getting your heart
shattered and
then trying to
mend it yourself,
holding every single piece
and putting it back
together again
in hope that
the next person
who comes along
would cherish it
more than
the one who broke it.

I gave you
everything
and you,
you could not even
keep a promise.

You can tell her
that she is beautiful
over and over
and over again
but tell her
just once that
she is not worthy
and she will
remember it
over and over
and over again.

Tell me
was I just
another bridge
for you to
walk all over?

I have forgotten
what it is like
to be gentle
with my heart.

If he truly
wanted to be with you
he would not
have left you,
it really is as simple
as that.

I read the words
'I still love you'
and I swear
I thought
I was supposed
to feel something.

We hold onto
things that hurt us
just because
they make us
happy.

- a paradox.

I fall too hard
too quickly
and that is
my biggest
problem.

I am so tired
of being that
person,
the one that
always gets
left behind.

I wish I could convince you
that what you feel
is not love,
it is nothing
close to it
I wish I could show you
what it means to fall in love
but sometimes
I do not remember it myself.

My feelings are
too transparent
sometimes
and I do not know
if that is
a blessing
or a curse.

We play too many games
with our hearts
and then we wonder why
they fail to take us
seriously.

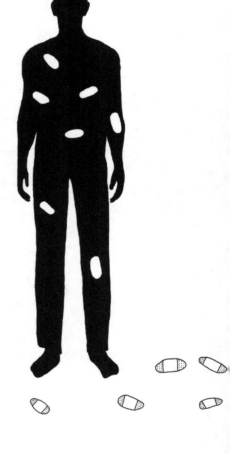

I broke myself
and used
every single piece
trying to fix you,
you will break yourself
trying to forget me.

You gave away
all of your
I love you's
to a man who
was only worthy
of your
goodbyes.

To the ones
who hurt me
who tore me down
who broke me
until there was nothing
but my dignity
holding me together,
to the ones
who taught me
that I should never
love, trust or care
selflessly,
to the ones who left me,

today I thank you.

the healing.

Let me tell you a little bit about healing. There you are, standing at the edge of the highest mountain with your fists held tightly by your sides as you stare at what lies before you. It is darkness. The air is calm and a soft wind brushes against your skin and you sway your head in the direction it takes you, bristling thick strands of your hair that smells of the sweet-strawberry shampoo that you soaked it in that morning because you care about how you look. And what you feel. And the things that your mind was telling you every step along the way towards that tall mountain facing an empty blackness that will suck you in and throw you back out as though you are nothing but a thin crinkle of dust. You also care about every single thing that you said to your reflection in the mirror in the morning when, once more you woke up with a grateful smile as the sun was beating down on a face that had a good night's sleep. And as you scrolled through a succession of messages you received from your family and friends and people who love and care about you on your phone, you took a bite of toast and sipped the coffee you made yourself that morning, just like every other morning. Those positive talks to your glowing face in the mirror mean everything to you now as you stare at the edge of this mountain of lost feelings and wishes and ideas and once-held dreams that you had created for yourself. And you think about every single thing that you have to be grateful for as you stand at the edge of the highest mountain with your fists held tightly by your sides as you stare at what lies before you. It is darkness. And you let yourself fly.

The healing
hurts a lot more
than
the falling.

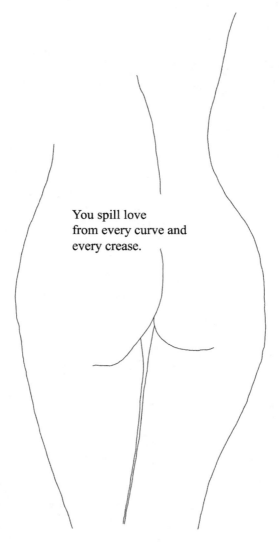

You spill love
from every curve and
every crease.

Somehow
he turns
even the bad days
into days I wish
never ended.

And you will always be
too much
for some people,
too kind
too friendly
too sensitive
too giving
too loud
too quiet
too hopeful
too loving
too fierce
too passionate
too scared
too soft
too rigid
too much of this and
too much of that
too much of every sin-
gle thing that makes
you the person that you are,
do not change yourself because
you are too much
for people who
are too little,
just remember
your too much
will never make sense
to those who put boundaries
where there should be none.

I have written away
my sorrows
more times than
I can remember.

Dearest,
I see you
sitting there
dressed in solemnity
bathed in light
with eyes that
show me
you are carrying
the weight of
all your worries
on your back
and still you smile,
still you smile.

I find warmth
and comfort
in my own arms.

I will always love
how sometimes
we do not need
to share words
in order to share
feelings,
we just need to share
a gaze.

And in the end it was you,

when those you loved left
when those who never
loved you did not turn
back even once
to look at you
when they hurt you
just because they could,
you were the one who picked
up your own pieces
you were the one
who brought the glue
to join them back together
to mend yourself
to stop your heart
from breaking
those you trusted
never came to save you,
in the end it was you.

Some things are
better left unsaid,
expressing
how I feel
about you
is not one of them.

I forgave you
not because
you deserved it
but because
I no longer had
room in my heart
for hatred.

Darling,
you need to trust
your healing process,
you are exactly where
you are supposed to be
in your journey.

In this lifetime
will I ever
come across someone
who will naturally
see through
this flesh and bone
straight into my soul,
will I?

I missed you
even before I
met you.

- *to my future.*

Darkness seems
to run away from
me these days
and I am okay,
starless nights
were never meant
for dreamers anyway.

Talk to me in darkness
in the fragile hours
between night and day
talk to me in whispers
with your eyes closed and
your mouth inches away,
talk to me in darkness
because that is where
I will hear what you
have to say.

Love is gentle
in the strongest way.

And the only way
to fight every battle
in your life
and the only way
to deal with the pain
and the only way
to heal
change
and grow
is to be there for yourself
because you need you.

To every man who thought
I was completely ordinary,

you only saw what
I chose to show you
because
I wanted you to be
disinterested
I hid away the best parts
and painted a picture of dullness
for you to meet,
you thought you had
me all figured out
you thought there was
nothing to see
you never realised that I was
hiding the extraordinary
within me
because I felt you were
never worthy of me.

If I love you

I will tell you that I do
whenever I feel it throbbing
inside my chest and I cannot
keep it in any longer,
I will give you all of my time
because when you love someone
you can never be too busy for them,
I will speak to you whenever I
need you and whenever
you need me because

If I love you

I will be there for you like
a best friend
like a lover
I will make promises that
I can keep and
I will never make you wait for
my attention because you will
deserve every ounce of it
and more,

If I love you

I will give you all of me
in exchange for nothing
but love from you
I will not view your heart as
a trophy that I need to win
instead I will cherish your heart
and keep it safe,

And if I love you

I will never take your love
for granted
in loving you
I will learn to love myself
and that will be
the biggest gift of all.

Do not look
into my eyes
my feelings
will show.

You
        are
              the
                    reason
                            why
                      I still
                  believe
              in
goodness.

And each day I pray for
one thing
and one thing only,
to become a far better
person today than I was
yesterday
and to become a far
better person tomorrow
than I am today.

Some nights
the hurting
becomes
the healing.

I cannot change what happened
but I can promise you this
things will get better
the sun will shine
your tears will quieten
your heart will not hurt
and everything will slowly
fall back into place
even better than before.

And somehow
I keep finding myself
wrapped up
in thoughts of you,
just tell me how
to untangle myself.

How beautiful it is
to be loved
for your
broken parts
to be loved
only for
your broken parts.

Some days
are better than others.

Women who write
about heartache
and pain
are not waiting
to be saved
we have the strength
to write about a pain
that we managed to
save ourselves from,
we managed to find
our own way.

I trust you,
this is me handing
you my soul
hoping that
you will give me
yours in exchange.

I will not believe
it is love
until I can
feel it in my
bones.

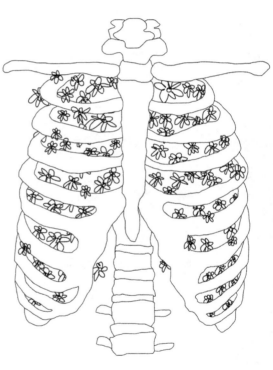

This is for
every single person
who broke me
and showed me that
broken was not the way
I was supposed to feel,
this is for
every single person
who hurt me
and made me realise
that through help-
ing myself
I was supposed to heal.

I
am
in
awe
of
you.

Believe me
you are not
your mistakes
your regrets
those hard
lessons learnt
nor every little
thing that brings
you down,
you never were.

Certain people
will come into
in your life one day
who will give you so
much happiness,
love and care
making you
wonder
just where
they were
all this time and
why you did not
meet them sooner.

I went through hell
just to realise
my worth
and I am not
going to forget
it again.

You were there
to embrace me
when the world
had failed me.

I will always love
how
sometimes
we do not need
to share words
in order to share
feelings,
we just need to share
a gaze.

I will never justify myself
for feeling.

Give love,
as much love as
you have within you
to give to him,
give him your kindness
your warmth
the passion within you
without expecting
it to find its way
back to you,
but it will
my darling
it will come back to you
one day
so just give love
and keep on giving.

And sometimes
people will look at you
and say that
you are 'too nice'
as if it is an insult
you need to remember
that you are not
being 'too nice' to anyone,
you are simply
being human
in a world
filled with people
who have forgotten
humanity.

I cannot become
a woman I am not
for the sake of
someone else's love
and that is where
I fail
every single time.

How do you go back
to being the best part
of the person
you once were
while holding on
to the best part
of what you
have become?

In the end
they will try to tell you
how to feel
what to think
where to go
in the end
they will try to give you
a reason to break
a reason to grieve
a reason to fear
and in the end
they will come back to you
to ask for forgiveness
to make amends
and that is when you will know
what they were worth
and what you are worth.

You gave me
your hand
to hold but I
placed my heart
on it instead.

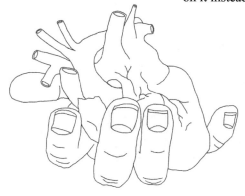

I wish that
one day you heal
that when your face smiles
your soul smiles with you,

I wish that
one day you feel happy
on the inside and
positivity touches
your core,

I wish that
one day your heart
stops hurting and
his memories fade away
and you learn that you
deserve the best that
life gives you
and nothing less,

and I wish that
one day you give love
another chance
where you open your
heart and soul to another
person one more time
one last time
because love needs you to,

just this once
just this once.

Out of the many possible
worlds in which I could
have been
I landed in the one
where I met you.

I will preach
about women empowerment
and equal rights and
the importance of
my individual identity
and my worth
and my inner beauty
and my strength
and how invaluable
every single thing
that makes me a woman is
but at the same time
I cannot help but smile
when he holds the door
open for me
or pushes my chair out
or hands me his coat
when I am feeling cold
and I do not know
if the woman within me
should rage in anger
or melt in love.

- *constantly torn.*

Give yourself
the benefit of doubt.

My heart feels empty
my mind is numb
I feel content
and lost
at the same time,
I know what I want
from my life
but then again
I could not be
more unsure.

You make me
want to believe
in love
again.

You did not
come to the
earth
to live a life
for others
so why do you
let their
opinions
of you
affect you?

And sometimes
ignorance is the best
way to deal with
your heart,
what it does not know
will not kill it.

Writing
does not come
as easily
as it used to,
these days
I try so hard to
remember
what it felt like to
once love you
when those days
loving you was all
I had ever known.

Be your own strength
your own light
your own hero
and you will never
need another
to save you again.

I know you gave him
your everything
but just because
he could not give you
what you deserved in return
it does not mean
that someone else will not,
your ability to love
cannot diminish
with just one heartbreak.

In a world that is only
one among many others
sheltering more than
7 billion people in
innumerable countries
cities, towns and villages
who cross paths with
one another at various
points in their lives,
I refuse to believe
that meeting you was
just a coincidence.

This is for every time
you thought you would not
see the sun again,
this is for every time
you felt the need
to justify yourself
for hurting
for hoping
for grieving,

this is for every cold
night spent alone
and in tears
without believing
that you would ever
come out from it,

this is for your journey
from heartbreak to healing
from darkness to light
from cold to warmth
from his painful love
to the softness
of your own arms,

this is for you.

It is your depth
that scares them
the most.

If I care about you
as my family
my friend
or as a lover
I will bare my soul
place it in my palm
and hand it over to you
because I do not believe
in giving someone I love
just a part of me
that is not the whole me.

You can
kindle her skin
with your touch
but you can never
kindle her soul.

What are vulnerabilities?

They are the
things we keep
close to us
for fear that if
we reveal them
then it will be
easier for others
to hurt us,
then is our heart not
our biggest vulnerability?

So ask yourself this question,
why are you scared
to show others
your vulnerabilities
when you show them
your heart
through your eyes
every single day.

You may enter
a poet's life
as a person
but you will
always leave
as a poem.

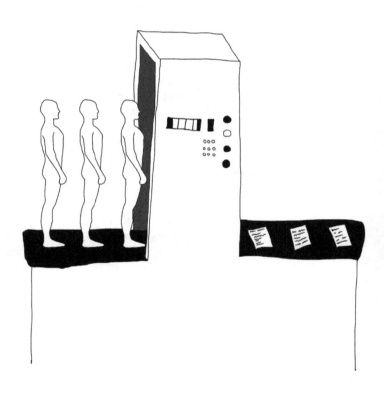

I will keep you
in my prayers
before I sleep
tonight
and that is
the biggest gift
I could ever give
anyone.

There is nothing wrong
with love being
quiet and calm
slow and steady
distant from the world
and everyone within it,

there is nothing wrong
with love starting
from two people and
remaining between them.

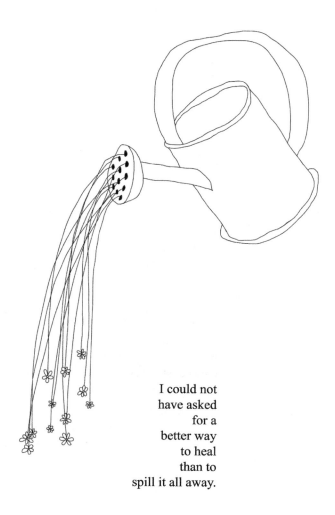

I could not
have asked
for a
better way
to heal
than to
spill it all away.

And within
every person
there are a million
emotions beating
that they are hearing
that they are feeling
that they are hurting
to keep inside
but they are still beating,
they are still beating.

I look at you
and find every
single thing
that I had been
searching for
in a single
human being,
and I am scared,
believe me
I am so scared.

Hold on to
things that
cause you pain
and try to find
your strength
in them.

No two moments
are the same
and a person in
those two moments
definitely is not,
so if you came back to me
with the hope
that you would get
the girl you left behind,
then I am sorry
she is no longer here
because the moment
you left,
she went with you.

And that is the problem
with writing such poems,
either they will
think that you are
helplessly heartbroken
or they will
think that you are
hopelessly in love.

It was *(not)* meant to be,

the most
simplistic way
to explain
what happens when
things go right *(wrong)*
which we would otherwise
spend our whole lives
trying to understand.

Give me everything

your smile
your laughter
the gleam in your eyes
your dreams
your goals
the things that
keep you up at night,

Give me everything

your hopes
your fears
every time you shed tears
those secrets that you hide
your lows
your highs,

Give me everything

your kindness
your will
your heart
your soul
every time you feel
every time you hurt,

Give me everything

and in exchange
I will give my
everything to you.

Be brave enough
to love yourself first.

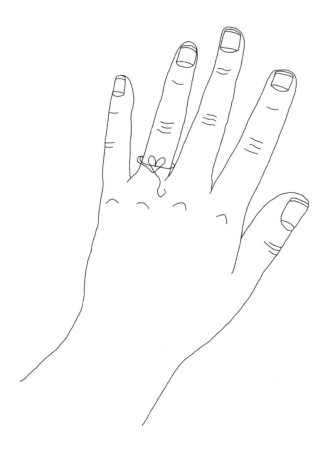

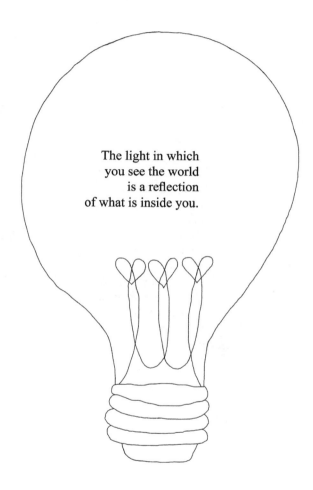

The light in which
you see the world
is a reflection
of what is inside you.

Please, do not assume
that you know
what is going on in a
poet's heart
through reading her poems
when you cannot
if a lot of the time
even I am confused
about the relationship
between what I feel
and what I write.

The day you meet
someone
who understands
your silence
better than your words
who reads your eyes
better than your lips
who knows your scars
better than you do,
hold on to them
and never let them go.

I swear
I would be lying
if I said
I have met
someone like you
before.

God gave you
two hands
two feet
two eyes
two ears
but one heart
to tell you
that you cannot fit
two people
where there should
only be one.

He taught me
how to love myself
and I taught him
how to love.

It is a constant cycle of
breaking and healing
hurting and feeling
fixing and mending
this journey
is never ending.

I have stopped
trying to understand
the reason why
we all break
maybe there is one which
explains why we step foot in
each other's lives
guiding the way
or changing the direction
of the person we are affecting,
the purpose is not to understand
why we break one another,
the purpose is to understand
what we learn from it.

My only mistake was
that I should have been
the best version of me
for me
but I was too busy
trying to be
the best version of me
for you.

The hardest part
is not
the falling
the feeling
the hoping
or
the hurting,
it is always
the grieving.

I know I am falling
deep into the
ocean of love
knowing that
this time
I will not be able
to save myself
but still,
I am falling
I am falling
I am falling,

I have fallen.

The most important thing
pain ever taught me
was the art of
knowing when
to say 'no'.

Writers hold onto
the things that
break them
longer than they should
because they are scared
that if they lose
the feeling of pain
then they might lose
the art that comes with it too.

And after
the hurt
the pain
the scars
the tears and
every moment
of uncertainty
about its existence,
love will come back
to you,
it always does.

You saved me
from the darkness
and I saved you
from yourself.

I
  keep
    tumbling
   in
and
   out
     of
      love
       with
        myself.

In the end
I am just glad that
I managed to
hold onto my sanity
through it all.

He showed me that
there is so much of me
to love
and I forgot what
that felt like.

I came home to myself
the day I wrote you away.

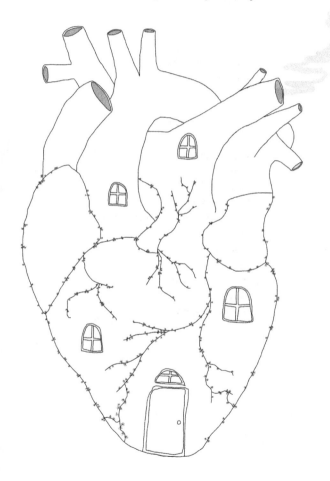

She wanted a house that
stayed with her
close to her heart
wherever she would go
a house that was there
to love
to protect
to hold forever
a house that did not
feel foreign
it was as comfortable
as her own skin
a house that was
hers to keep
it was her own,
so she created a home
within herself.

I hope you
find it within you
to forgive every single person
who hurt you
who made you feel low
who caused tears in eyes that
only reflected light
and I hope you
find it within you
to pray for their wellbeing
to never let bitterness
cloud your mind
to never let negativity
darken your heart
and I hope you
find it within you
to keep loving despite being
taught that love kills
because you know
you are worthy
because you know
you deserve love
you always have been,

regardless of what they said
regardless of what they did.

About The Author

Ruby Dhal is a poetess, writer and aspiring novelist currently residing in the UK. As a young child, Ruby used books as a form of escapism from painful experiences of the real world. As she grew older she realised that books were meant to take her closer to reality and brought her at one with her true self. Through reading and writing poetry, she discovered herself and walked on a new path through which she learned about self-love and revival, and she then sought out to do the same for others. Her passion for writing and revealing countless emotions for the world to share in has allowed Ruby to receive an endless amount of love and support from a generous social media following. Her first book was extremely well-received by her readers and her second book is an attempt to go further and allow her readers to take a new journey through love and heartbreak with the purpose of healing and discovering one's true depths. When Ruby isn't writing poetry she is working on her first novel which is based on many true events that have taken place in her life. You can find Ruby on Instagram (@r.dhalwriter), Facebook (@r.dhalwriter) and Twitter (rdhalwriter).

Acknowledgements

To my mother. I know you're out there somewhere watching me with a kind smile and that gleam in your big brown eyes that had the power to melt even the stonehearted. And I want to thank you. I want to thank you for bringing me into this world and passing down all of your values to me despite me being unfortunate enough not to have grown under your wing. I want to thank you for blessing me with your heart, although I've been told it is a little too soft sometimes, for blessing me with your eyes, they're beautiful – I've been told countless times – and for blessing me from wherever your throne is resting every single day. I love you and I always will.

To my father. Thank you for holding my hand when the love of your life left it. Thank you for teaching me everything from how to ride a bike, to how to stand up for myself and to the more valuable lessons of how to fight each battle in my life. Thank you for teaching me about strength, resilience and kindness. And thank you for loving me unconditionally. You are the reason why I am this woman today.

To my brother. Thank you for being the biggest blessing in my life. You are and always will be my saviour, my angel, the one who believed in me when I didn't even believe in myself and the sole reason for why I dream. You took care of me, you loved me and you supported me. You are the anchor of my ship and you will always be the one person I look up to more than anything. Despite it all, we made it through together and isn't that a wonderful thing?